D0882491

CALEDON PUBLIC LIBRARY

# HAIDA

ABORIGINAL PEOPLES OF CANADA

**Jennifer Nault**

Published by Weigl Educational Publishers Limited
6325 10 Street S.E.
Calgary, Alberta, Canada
T2H 2Z9

Website: www.weigl.com

Library and Archives Canada Cataloguing in Publication

Nault, Jennifer
          Haida : Aboriginal peoples of Canada / Jennifer Nault.
(Aboriginal peoples of Canada)
Includes index.
ISBN 978-1-55388-506-1 (bound).--ISBN 978-1-55388-513-9 (pbk.)
          1. Haida Indians--Juvenile literature.  I. Title.
II. Series: Aboriginal peoples of Canada (Calgary, Alta.)
E99.H2N283 2009          j971.1004'9728          C2009-903518-9

Printed in the United States of America
1 2 3 4 5 6 7 8 9  13 12 11 10 09

Photograph and Text Credits

Cover: Getty Images ; Alamy: pages 6, 7, 10M, 11R, 13T, 21; Canadian Museum of Civilization: pages 9T (VII-B-1094, D2004-05845), 9M (VII-B-899, IMG2009-0063-0066-Dm), 9B (VII-B-1156 a,b, D2002-002706), 13B (VII-B-162 a, D2002-000673), 16B; Corbis: pages 8, 12, 14, 15, 16, 20, 23; CP Images: page 4; Getty Images: pages 1, 5, 10L, 10R, 11L, 11M, 17.

Every reasonable effort has been made to trace ownership and to obtain permission to reprint copyright material. The publishers would be pleased to have any errors or omissions brought to their attention so that they may be corrected in subsequent printings.

All of the Internet URLs given in the book were valid at the time of publication. However, due to the dynamic nature of the Internet, some addresses may have changed, or sites may have ceased to exist since publication. While the author and publisher regret any inconvenience this may cause readers, no responsibility for any such changes can be accepted by either the author or the publisher.

We gratefully acknowledge the financial support of the Government of Canada through the Book Publishing Industry Development Program (BPIDP) for our publishing activities.

**PROJECT COORDINATOR**  Heather Kissock

**DESIGN**  Terry Paulhus, Kenzie Browne

**ILLUSTRATOR**  Martha Jablonski-Jones

# Contents

# The People

The Haida are a **First Nation**. Most Haida live off the west coast of British Columbia on a group of islands called Haida Gwaii. Some Haida live in Alaska.

In the past, their island location made it easy for the Haida to thrive. The climate was warm, and many plants and animals were found in the area. The Haida had steady access to natural resources, such as trees, birds, and fish. Their surroundings provided the Haida with all they needed to survive.

## NET LINK

To learn more about Haida Gwaii, go to **www.haidaheritagecentre.com/ location.html**.

# Haida Homes

## LONGHOUSES

In the past, the Haida lived in longhouses. These houses were longer than they were wide. The houses were lined up in rows along the beach. The chief's house was in the middle.

Each longhouse had one firepit. There were no windows, so the Haida made a hole in the roof for smoke to go through. A board was propped up to protect the opening of the hole from leaks.

Haida longhouses were made from red cedar. Some houses had a doorway that featured a **totem pole**. Very few longhouses exist today. Most Haida live in houses and apartment buildings.

# Haida Clothing

## CAPES

Haida men and women often covered themselves with capes. Some capes were made from cedar bark. Others were made from elk skin. The capes were sometimes decorated with paint and fringes.

## SKIRTS, TUNICS, AND LEGGINGS

Both men and women wore tunics, or shirts, to cover the top half of their bodies. For the bottom half of their bodies, the men wore leggings, and the women wore skirts. These clothes were often made from woven strips of cedar bark.

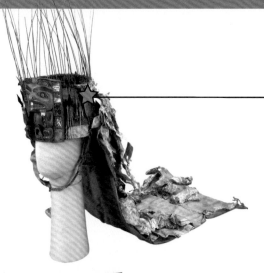

## HEADDRESSES

Chiefs wore headdresses for special ceremonies. On their forehead, they would wear a carved wooden **plaque** called a frontlet.

## HATS

The Haida wove hats from the roots of spruce trees. These hats had broad rims to protect the Haida from sunlight. The Haida often painted animal designs onto their hats.

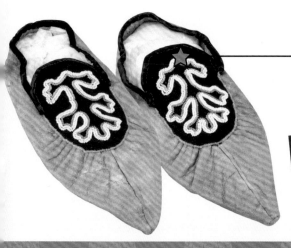

## MOCCASINS

In cold weather, the Haida would wear leather moccasins on their feet. If the weather was warm, they went barefoot.

# Hunting and Gathering

## SALMON

Salmon was the Haida's main food. To **preserve** the fish, it was smoked. This meant it was hung over a fire to dry.

## HALIBUT

Halibut was another fish that the Haida caught. Halibut was often used to make soups and stews.

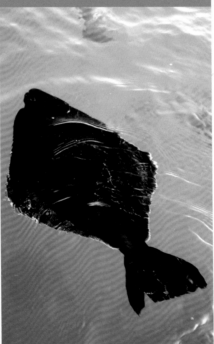

## BERRIES

The Haida picked berries for food. Some berries were eaten fresh, while others were cooked and dried in the form of cakes.

The Haida lived close to the Pacific Ocean. Most of their food came from the ocean, but they hunted animals found on the islands as well. The Haida also gathered the many food plants that grew there.

## CLAMS

The Haida dug clams from the beach to eat. The clams were removed from their shells and smoked.

## DEER

The Haida hunted land animals. Deer were found throughout the area. They were used for food and clothing.

## WHALES

The Haida hunted whales for their meat and oil. Whale oil made a good dipping sauce and was used to store berries.

# Haida Tools

## FISHING RAKES

The Haida used many tools to catch fish. Two of the main tools used were rakes and weirs. Rakes were large forks made of wood or bone. A line connected the fork to a wooden pole. The Haida held the wooden pole and threw the fork in the water to spear the fish.

Haida fishing lines were made from cedar bark and spruce roots.

## WEIRS

Weirs are fence-like structures. The Haida stretched them across a stream. Fish would get caught in the weirs. Traps, hooks, lines, and spears were other tools used to catch fish. To hunt land animals, the Haida used spears as well as bows and arrows.

# Moving from Place to Place

**CANOE** The Haida relied on water for most of their travel. They would use canoes when fishing and visiting other villages. They also used canoes to transport them into battles with other First Nations.

Each canoe was carved from a single cedar tree. Some canoes could fit up to 60 paddlers.

## NET LINK
Find out how the Haida built their canoes at **www.suite101.com/article.cfm/canada_for_kids/114339**.

# Haida Music and Dance

The Haida made music with drums, rattles, and their voices. Drums were held in one hand. A stick was used to beat the drum. Rattles added a swishing sound to the music of the drums. They were meant to sound like salmon moving through the water.

The Haida often sang and danced to the sounds of drums and rattles. Their songs and dances told stories about Haida life and history. When dancing, the Haida wore masks that represented characters in the story. The Haida still perform these dances today.

# The Coming of the Salmon

The Coming of the Salmon story explains how the salmon came to live so close to the Haida.

The Chief's daughter was crying for a great, shining fish. Her father wanted to find the fish for her, but no one had ever seen a fish as she described. He decided to ask Raven to find this great fish.

When the Chief called Raven and told him of his problem, Raven stated that he knew the fish well. He flew off, promising that he would bring the fish to the village.

Raven flew until he spotted a group of salmon in the waters below him. He dived down and grabbed one. He then headed back to the Haida village.

By chance, Raven had caught the son of the Salmon Chief. The Salmon Chief wanted his son back. He and his subjects followed Raven.

When Raven returned to the village, he gave the salmon to the Chief's daughter. She stopped crying and was happy. Raven then told the Haida to string a net across the river because many more salmon were coming. When the salmon arrived at the village, they were caught in the net. Every year since, salmon have returned to the waters near the village.

Art and decoration were part of everything the Haida created. The main style of decoration used black outlines to create designs. These outlines were then filled in with red paint. Totem poles, masks, and houses all followed this style of decoration.

Haida items were often decorated with **spiritual** images and crests. Crests included figures of animals, birds, and sea creatures.

### NET LINK

To see examples of Haida art, go to **www.virtualmuseum.ca/Exhibitions/Haida/java/english/art/art2i.html**.

# Make a Haida Mask

**Materials**
Computer
Construction paper
Paint or felt markers, in black, red, blue, and green
Scissors
Pieces of fur, leather, or shells (optional)
Two pieces of string
Mirror

1. Research Haida masks on the Internet by typing "Haida" and "mask" into a search engine, such as Google. Pick a mask you would like to make.
2. Cut a large, oval circle out of construction paper. It should be large enough to cover your whole face.
3. Cut holes in the paper for your eyes to look through. Cut a hole for your mouth as well.
4. Colour, and decorate your mask.
5. Carefully attach two pieces of string, one on each side of the mask. Tie your mask to your head, and look in the mirror to see yourself.

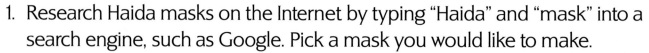

**First Nation:** a member of Canada's Aboriginal community who is not Inuit or Métis

**plaque:** a flat plate or slab that is decorated

**preserve:** to keep food from rotting

**spiritual:** sacred or religious

**totem pole:** a large, upright pole that is carved and painted with First Nations emblems